REFLECTIONS

My Solo Travels *from* Fear to Wonder

Linda Lee

REFLECTIONS

My Solo Travels
from Fear to Wonder

Photography: Linda Lee

Developmental Editors:
Mila Johansen, From Pen to Published
Margaret Campbell, ITW Group Inc

First Edition April 2025

ISBN 978-1-952508-17-2

HopeWithHelpers@gmail.com
HopeWithHelpers.com

COUNTRIES AND PROVINCES I'VE VISITED

Aruba	England	Mexico
Austria	France	Monaco
Bahamas	Germany	Netherlands
Belgium	Grand Cayman Island	Norway
Belize	Greece	Palestine
Canada	Greenland	Poland
Cyprus	Ireland	Scotland
Czech Republic	Israel	Sweden
Denmark	Italy	Switzerland
Ecuador	Jamaica	Turkey
Egypt	Liechtenstein	USA

The Van de Sande Family: Geert, Trees, Maaike, and Frits welcomed me at age 16, a foreign exchange student, to join their Dutch family.

Submerge into crystal, salty water. Oh, how life dances below.
Snorkeling in Oranjestad, Aruba

RECESS IS BACK

An Invitation
to adventure, everywhere possible…

Surround yourself in natures essence
Be surprised by
lacy white flickers of light
all around you

Surrender on green grass, grounding
Be present for all the critters
playing with you

Partake in Wonder
Trails and unexpected waterfalls
Plunge your feet, absorb its force
Soak in its power

Imagine being carried on a horse, bareback
discovering an *Old Forest*
Their magnificence will counsel
in whispers floating on wind

Submerge into crystal salty waters
Oh, how life dances below
Welcome many watching you, watching them
They are attuned
with Sources energy
Effortlessly

Will you Come out and Play too?
Recess is Back, Calling you

ARE YOU WILLING

Are you willing to receive

Are you willing to embrace change

Are you willing to center into your heart

Are you willing to receive from the unexpected

Are you willing to offer love and a smile to your Reflection

"Through each experience
there is a hidden treasure."

Linda Lee

Welcome, I am Linda. Come play with me and enter into a blissful world of travel and nature's whispers.

Autoire, France

Thank you so much for opening my book!

A heartfelt blend of conversations between my photos, poems and nature I had filed away for far too long. It is time to share them.

My journey into travel and nature's wisdom began as a little girl. During the summer months I would lose myself in the woods for hours. I felt connected to everything around me, paying close attention to hear whispers and receive vivid details that activated all my senses. I took snapshots within my mind of all the beauty before me. I found courage to be on my own and the only time I felt playful and free to be me. I also knew I needed to find a way to escape my childhood home.

I loved going to my school library looking through picture books of the world dreaming page after page. From the ancient pyramids in Egypt, to Dutch culture, their windmills, wooden shoes, and cheese. I felt as if I belonged there. A joy to look at those books, the faraway places full of art, their history and the unknown.

Connecting in nature and looking at those picture books gave me something to look forward to. I closed my eyes and wished with all my heart I would travel to those places one day. My Angels answered at the age of 16 and presented a way. There was a poster in the library offering an opportunity to live abroad as a foreign exchange student. I grabbed that chance and thus a Solo Traveler I became.

I couldn't believe I was chosen by a Dutch family. I packed a suitcase, my Kodak Instamatic camera and braved getting on the plane. My Dutch family greeted me at the Amsterdam airport and introduced me to their culture and all the yumminess of something new. While there, the family and I went on a holiday (that's what they call vacation) to Germany, Austria and Belgium.

I fell deeply in love with my Dutch family and meeting new people that forged a lifetime of friendships. A passion blossomed for capturing beauty behind the camera lens in every country. I never imagined how that experience would change me forever. I felt ALIVE!

I learned early on how to be a Solo traveler on my own, without feeling alone. I have traveled most of the world Solo and met people everywhere that opened their doors and hearts, with a welcomed hug or kiss on the cheek.

I hope my book will inspire those who may be pensive of travel, especially Solo, to turn that fear into WONDER as I show you enchanted places I have been so far. I ask you to envision yourself with me page after page as I lend you my eye and written words showing you all the beauty, I see in everything. My journals, tiny stories they are, Reflections expressed through my poems.

During my travels, local or abroad, I was grateful for those pieces of my woundedness to be filled with excitement! By simply walking out my front door spontaneous or planned, the unexpected showed up with an opportunity to connect with life, that danced its way creatively through me.

I believe with every fiber of who I am, empowering possibilities, is where the magic begins. With pure intension, to give you a reason, something positive to hold onto, waiting to blossom from you and say I am ALIVE!

I am proud to share I have lived in The Netherlands, France, Norway, Sweden and Ireland. I have also visited 27 other countries and provinces. In the US, 48 states with North and South Carolina to be explored next.

I encourage you to get in your car with an overnight bag without a destination and go Play, by bus, train, ship or plane and yes, even a camel. I found there is always a safe place to land. I am convinced, by simply walking out your own front door, there is goodness around every corner and yumminess too.

In Grace,

Linda Lee

POEMS & IMAGES

POEMS & IMAGES

THE SEARCH

A Foreword by Tina Appenzellar

You embarked upon a journey
With a route planned
You knew that
"It had to start where it all began"

WHERE IT ALL BEGAN

This was your clue
You were being guided; this you knew to be true

You were asked to have
"Blind Faith"

Initially, you were blinded
by that which had yet to be revealed
FAITH is what brought you sight

BACK TO WHERE IT ALL BEGAN

To heal the negative effects of your childhood history
To find that YOU BELONGED to a family
On this search you found
Patience, Love
Expansion
an inner guidance to follow the signs
To listen to what your HEART tells you
The knowledge of "what keeps you safe"
A quieting of the manic mind
Inner strength
Mental Parking spaces

That it doesn't have to be done in one day
That you are special and brilliant
That it is safe to reveal your LIGHT
These discoveries carry you closer to your destiny
WHO YOU ARE WAS FOUND

AT WHERE IT ALL BEGAN

With so much love to our sisterhood
Love, Tina

Swans sashay through ripples from droplets of falling rain.
Annecy, France

I am filled with ribbons of color. I walked day after day to school,
crossing over the same bridge in Annecy, France.

DROPLETS OF FALLEN RAIN IN ANNECY

A gentle rain cascades upon a green canvas
that shelters the terrace in

Annecy

A table invites me
covered with white linen
to relax and find serenity in my view

I am filled with ribbons of color
that illuminate all my senses

"Bon jour" he smiles
"Une minute s'il vous plait" I requested
peeking at the menu

My appetite desires pommes frites
with a chilled glass of white wine

Un verre de Pinot Blanc is served
with an impressive plate of frites

Swans are perched on a ridge
alert while they groom
Others sashay through the ripples
from droplets of fallen rain

Life is quiet on the river Thiou
I relish all the beauty before me

"Ça va?" he asked
I hear sweetness in his voice
and happily, answer
"Oui"

ONE WITH THE ASPEN

I am glowing inside
listening to the trees
whisper to one another

A rustle of Aspen
unlike any sound I've ever heard

Looking up at the treetops
round leaves flickering
fancy thousands of butterfly wings

I observe the twinkling of a leaf
twirl within the wind

A distinctive creaking from a tree
Swaying back-and-forth

"Do we have your attention"

Come, sit with me called a Grand Aspen
I want to remind you of your childhood with us
I want to remind you of the earth below your feet
You belong amongst us

I have known this
thought it but a dream

Thank you for reminding me
to feel your roots and touch again
free to sway back-and-forth just like you

To walk off the beaten path, gives permission to be fully present.
Have a conversation with the eyes of the trees.
An Aspen Grove near Flagstaff, Arizona

I hear through a gust of wind showing its strength
Wherever you go connect with a tree
We are listening

I surrender into my chair
Grateful

Mute swans are everywhere floating in ponds and waterways,
orchestrating the perfect Symphony,

SWIRLS OF MOTION

They fly softly in the sky
creating remarkable patterns
Soaring to their own melody

Swirls of motion, one takes the lead
others follow in colors of gray and white

The sun reflects light with a glittering luster
orchestrating the perfect *Symphony*
for the pleasure of performing on tranquil water

Enchanting swans appear
feasting on cream colored grass

In unison, they immerse their sleek beaks
into the crisp cold stillness

Dew drops from an evening rain
grace their form

Together
Becoming one
They ease into slumber…

“Flawless
The essence of a woman...
Free to be Herself.”

Linda Lee

An image
is presented
she paused
it took
her breath
away
That's not
me
she said
Yes it is
Alka replied
Her eyes
welled
with tears
she feels.
flawless

Wisteria in full bloom bustling with bees. Autoire, France

A small village in France charmed my heart with all its allure and mystique.
Autoire, France

MY BELOVED AUTOIRE

Years, staring at a picture
I saw in a National Geographic magazine
drawn to it like a magnet, this small village in France
charmed my heart
with all its allure and mystique

I must experience this gem
In the Dordogne Region
I must...

I found myself walking
through French doors, feeling like a Princess
looking down onto the garden below
The crisp air filling
my lungs with an intoxicating aroma

Wisteria in full bloom bustling with bees
drapes its vine around the entrance
to a Château... Built in the 1600s

The topiaries are well groomed
A spectacular view with hidden surprises
guarded by an iron gate
waiting to entice me

The church bells ring, songbirds sing
a music I yearn to hear, sending me
right back to where my European soul belongs

A path calls
I am no longer staring at a picture from years ago
I am celebrating my beloved
Autoire

A sunbeam to highlight a new friend.

Freedom to dance any direction.

HOW LUCKY ARE YOU!

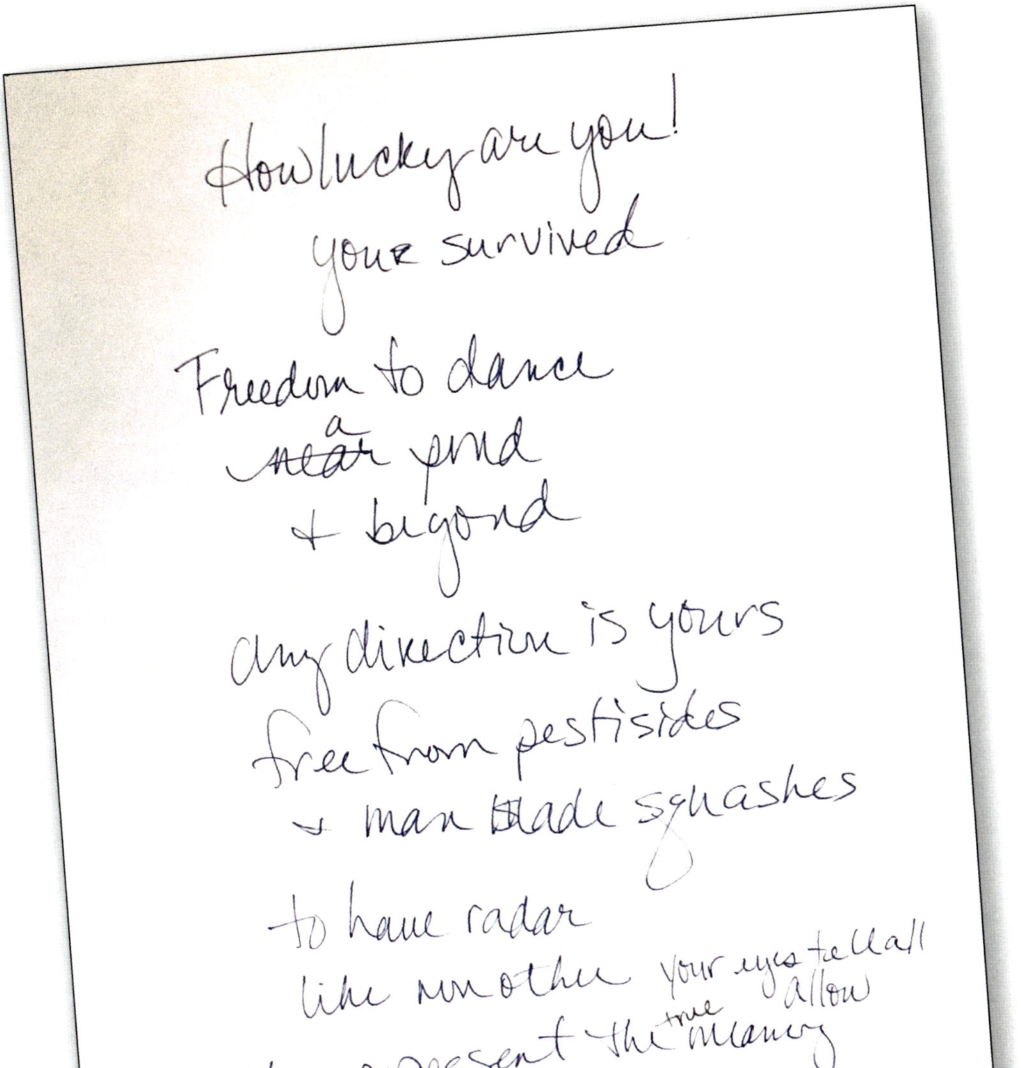

How lucky are you!
your survived

Freedom to dance
~~near~~ a pond
+ beyond

any direction is yours
free from pestisides
+ man made squashes

to have radar
like no other your eyes tell all
allow
You represent the true meaning
of "play"

A TIME TO PAUSE

A breath of wind offers a mist
from a stormy ocean below

Seagulls circle from high above
extending their wings to explore

Surrounded by trees buzzing with life
with tips of flickering palm leaves
The sun retreats
and twilight is upon them

A couple arrives
to a cottage nestled off in the distance

They lite a cobblestone fireplace
filling the room with a glow of autumn colors
influencing the romance

The flames fueled themselves
with repeated pops and snaps

A sofa beckons his body
he finds himself drawn to an oversized pillow
that cushions his fall as he surrenders

She wants to be near him
Passion takes over
as her body melts into his

Folded in each other's arms
laying against his strong chest
their lips engage in a kiss

Folded in each other's arms, their lips engage in a kiss.
A steamy romance off the shore in Aruba.

Maaike reflecting on her beloved Rwanda, Africa.

With fond memories of the Van de Sande family... my Dutch mother Trees, me, my Dutch sister Maaike, and my Dutch father Geert

MAAIKE, MY DUTCH SISTER

Reflecting on her beloved Rwanda
where she once stood
in a rainforest filled with gorillas, primates and trees

She contributed to a local village
teaching her expertise in
Animal Husbandry

A rustic simple lifestyle
where Maaike and Paul raised their children
amongst local tribes, nurturing memories

I imagined my Dutch sister
living with tribes in a foreign land
changed her
molded and shaped her into who she is

Or maybe it is me
flooded with memories of days long gone
Maaike's family welcomed me at 16
a foreign exchange student
changed me
molded and shaped me into who I am

Our story continues
our friendship and sisterhood blossoms
with memories of Mom, Pop and Brother Frits
Along with Paul, Sjors and Roos
and her grandchildren

Ik mis dorpin
Best, Nederland

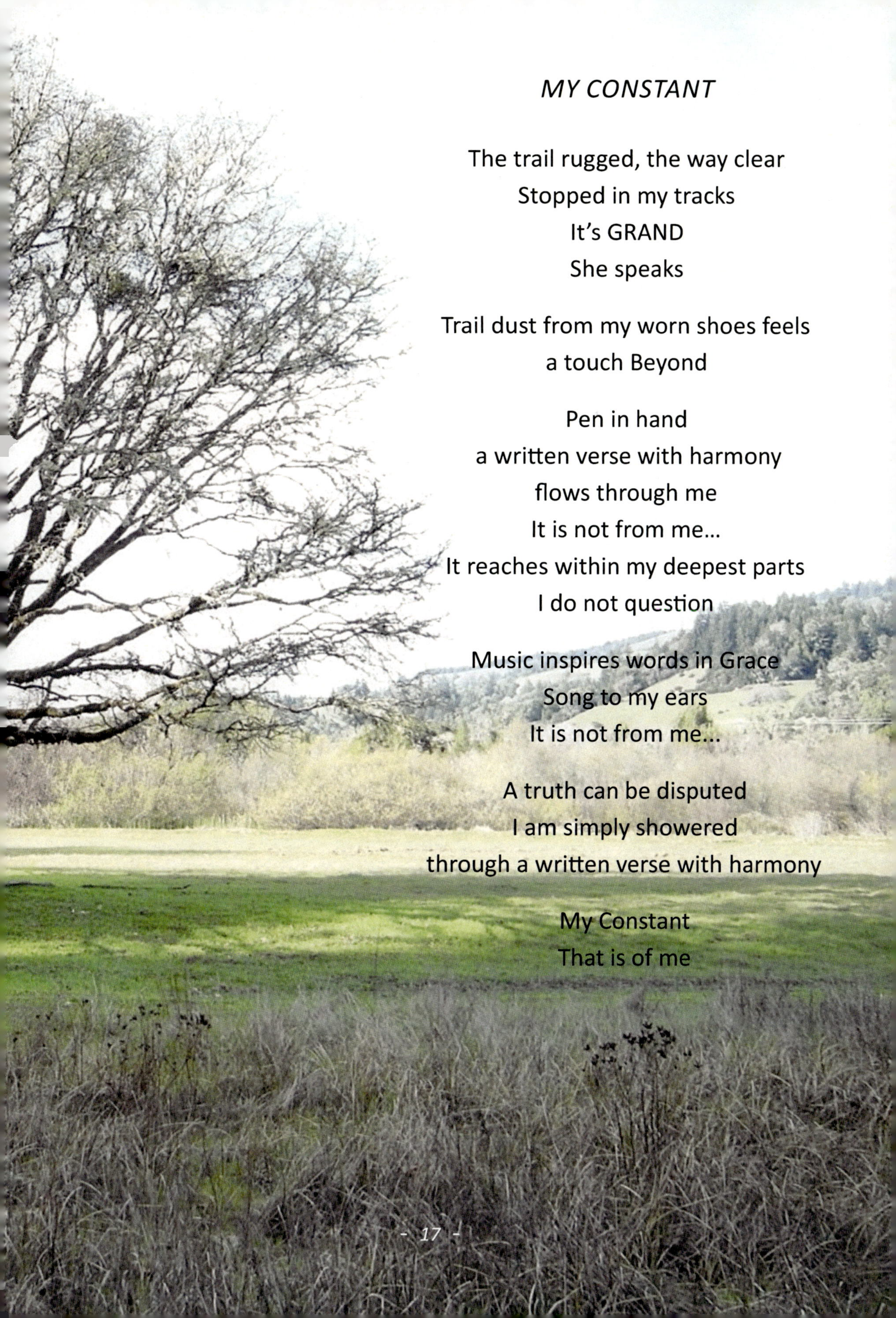

MY CONSTANT

The trail rugged, the way clear
Stopped in my tracks
It's GRAND
She speaks

Trail dust from my worn shoes feels
a touch Beyond

Pen in hand
a written verse with harmony
flows through me
It is not from me…
It reaches within my deepest parts
I do not question

Music inspires words in Grace
Song to my ears
It is not from me…

A truth can be disputed
I am simply showered
through a written verse with harmony

My Constant
That is of me

Enamoured with her presence in a graveyard.
Nice, France

Unspoken Breath

she seeks my attention
dusk absorbs her light
enamoured with her presence
a wave lands in my heart
in an unspoken breath
she whispers to my soul...

To witness a yellow butterfly glide between a chair and chain-link fences. Natures best.

AN EMPTY BALLET

I observe a radiant butterfly
simply taking in delight

Giving permission to memories
of my own dance

A spark no longer seen

Through the eyes of others
are glimpses into an empty ballet

I reflect, and continue to witness
a yellow butterfly glide
between a chair and chain-link fences

I pause to read an encouraging letter
written by my younger sister who writes like me
"I love you Nee, you're not alone"

A 300-year-old oak tree adds to its own
wave of pondering thoughts

His assuring faces offer
a distraction from my Frozen shoulders
which causes tremendous
stabbing physical pain

A Gregorian chime amplifies
a unique sound from ancient times
clearing any unwanted vibrations

I acknowledge the call
for a respite and give thanks
to all... with love

January 2007

Geese migration
Chico, California

My poem was inspired by an album I had purchased the night before.

I heard this song while watching the marshes flooded with ducks of all kinds.

My heart became flooded as well.

Song
The Emerald Way

By musical group
Two Thousand Two

FEATHERS ON THE MARSH

The sky is filled with flight
destination unknown

Flocks of webbed feet rest on soothing water
wings are stretched and flared

Others sing in various pitches
in a melody only they understand

The sun is fiery orange
steadily fading behind the mountain

Poised and content they float on the marsh
Nightfall is near

They are not alone-

Excitement from a shotgun
awakens any at rest

Many decide
to take flight can wait till dawn

They know...

To be close to a stingray, there is a trust that cannot be explained.
Grand Cayman Island

ELATION

I am Singing

Waving my arms
In the air

Shakin my Tooshie

Because I just don't care

Who might see me

I swam with Sharks
I swam with Stingrays
I swam with Dolphins

The Ocean with a rhythmic ease
She is the Soul
in this World

PURE ELATION

Swimming with Nurse Sharks, I am speechless. A fish head was tossed right in front of me. Thousands of serrated teeth opened to devour, glad it wasn't me!
Near the Barrier Reef, Belize

To feel the bond of a dolphin is an infectious joy to fall in love with.
Ocho Rios, Jamaica

She whispers "goodnight" as wooden shutters close to a sparkling Star filled eve.
Tende, a medieval village in the Alps-Maritimes in southeastern France.

FROM HER WINDOWSILL

Candlelight illuminates from a balcony
Colors are muted from dusk

Friends gather around a table
speaking joyfully in their native tongue

"Salut"
Wine glasses toast in celebration

She sits quietly on her windowsill
Eyes observing with envy

Shades of cobalt blue and sunflower yellow
adorn a beautiful fabric that lays beneath
an arrangement of wine bread and cheese

The crunch of a baguette
smooth texture of Camembert
intense zest of burgundy wine

She finds herself craving
all the flavors on her palette

Enjoying
every single morsel
within her mind

Candlelight begins to fade
Evening comes to an end

"Bonne nuit"
Spoken softly followed with
polite kisses expressed on welcomed cheeks

She whispers "goodnight"
as wooden shutters close to a sparkling
Star filled eve...

This elder Sequoia stretches skyward, open to sunny rays.
It's strength becomes something to celebrate.

Yummy memories of the cabin near Christopher Creek, Arizona

CAPTIVATED

A spider weaves its web
while swaying to a subtle breeze
touching its creation

I stand, captivated by its tapestry
of woven silk thread
A glimmer of sunlight pierces
through the spaces
the way it holds its own

Fern rise towards sunrays
touching each other
saying hello

Sounds of pine needle crunches
take me back to gleeful days
of summer, at the family cabin

My vision memorizes tree silhouettes
Their layers of bark
express to me
It's time -

The gypsy agrees

Like the spider
wherever life leads

Home is
within ...

How can it be? A yellow ladybug, indeed.
In my backyard in California.

RAINDROP KISSES

All is quiet in the courtyard

The birds take pause –
engaged from sunlight to sundown

Butterfly dances are sleeping
while dragonflies accelerate
in any direction of their choosing

Wildflowers from last year's planting
thrive in vibrational breezes

Deer discover a cool in the air
a pleasing relief from the heat

How can it be?
A yellow ladybug, indeed...

The garden, restoring
nourished by raindrop kisses

Surrender in a comfy chair
from an active day

Close my eyes
and imagine a light illuminating the room

Hello ... Soothing Source

Kariatides Temple 406 BC Athens, Greece.

IN GRACE

In the stillness of dawn
life begins to wake

Lights from the eve before
flicker
not quite ready to fade

Sunbeams rise from the horizon
simply to say
Welcome... A new day
A new way

Sunbeams rise from the horizon.
The Meteora Monasteries. 12th century Kalbaka, Greece

A song and dance around the corner
renewed with promise
giving expression to my creativity
through all divine gifts

Seen through eyes
pen to paper
transforms spirit into words
Not just words, but containers of energy

Doubt likes to rear its ugly head
to challenge
Not this time!!!

Free of worries for a moment
past, present or future
Concept is not an easy task

Yes... the body shouts
Adventure that resides within, come forth
Experience lands afar
wisdom from cultures and nature

A voice deep inside, a familiar kindness
Be Brave despite the chaos around you
Follow no Script
Give expression to your creative impulses
they are as natural as breath

Do not delay
Ask Source to make a way

Petals are soft velvet on tip of touch. Four Peaks Tonto National Forest, Arizona.

Hundreds of years stand before you. Four Peaks Tonto National Forest, Arizona.

A DESERT BALLAD

Life finds its way in this rugged
mountainous terrain

Cacti hold their own
in a desert filled with trails and rock

Tiny lizards wiggle up a branch
their skin well suited for
a blistering climate

A small chirp echoes from a nearby nest
hidden deep inside a Saguaro

Spring flowers in full bloom
an immense beauty
Petals are soft velvet on tip of touch

A butterfly, assisted by a gentle breeze
offers a flutter of wings across one's forehead
moving to its own rhythm

Hundreds of years stand before you
The desert has many a ballad
to share a story
for those who want

To be present

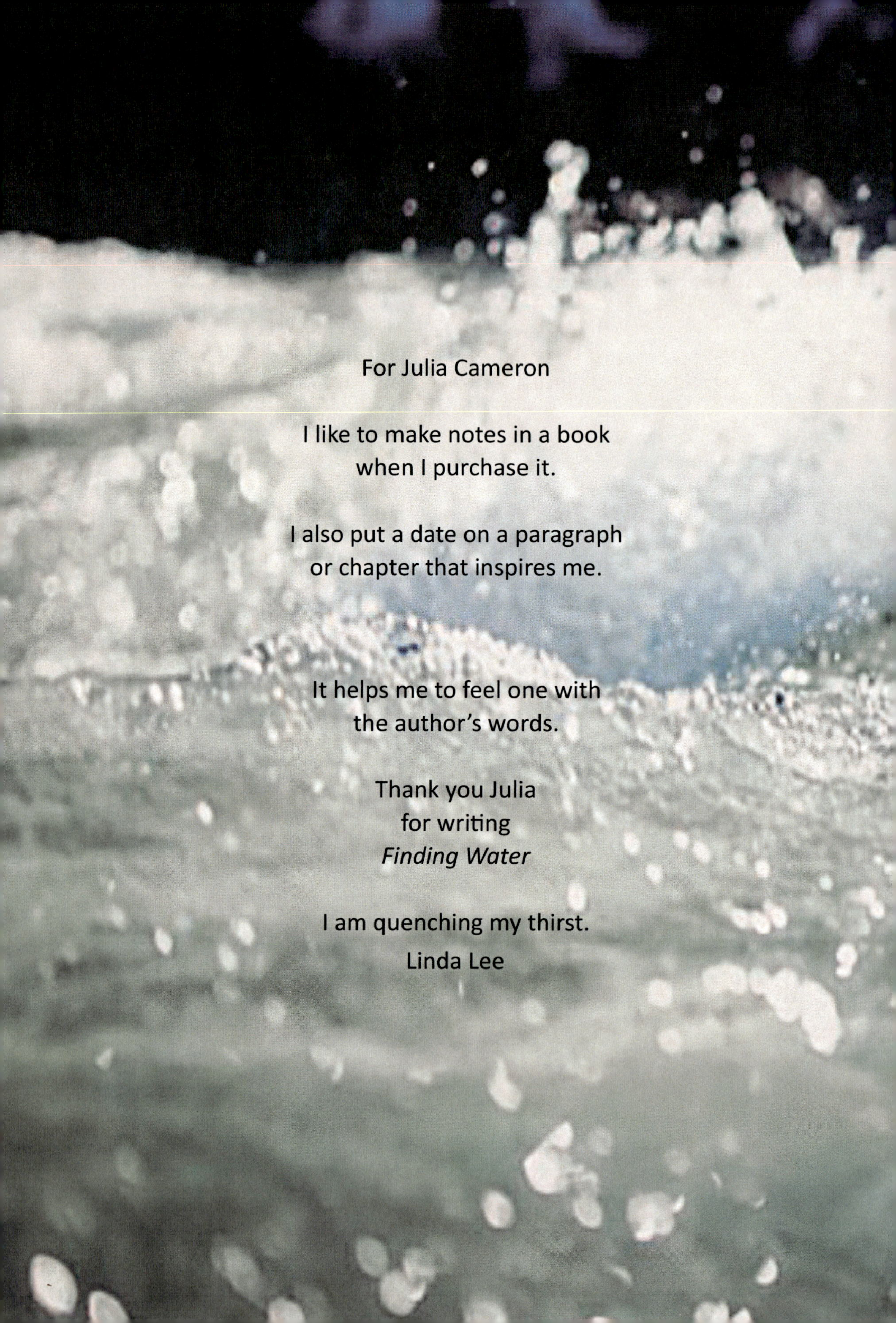

For Julia Cameron

I like to make notes in a book
when I purchase it.

I also put a date on a paragraph
or chapter that inspires me.

It helps me to feel one with
the author's words.

Thank you Julia
for writing
Finding Water

I am quenching my thirst.
Linda Lee

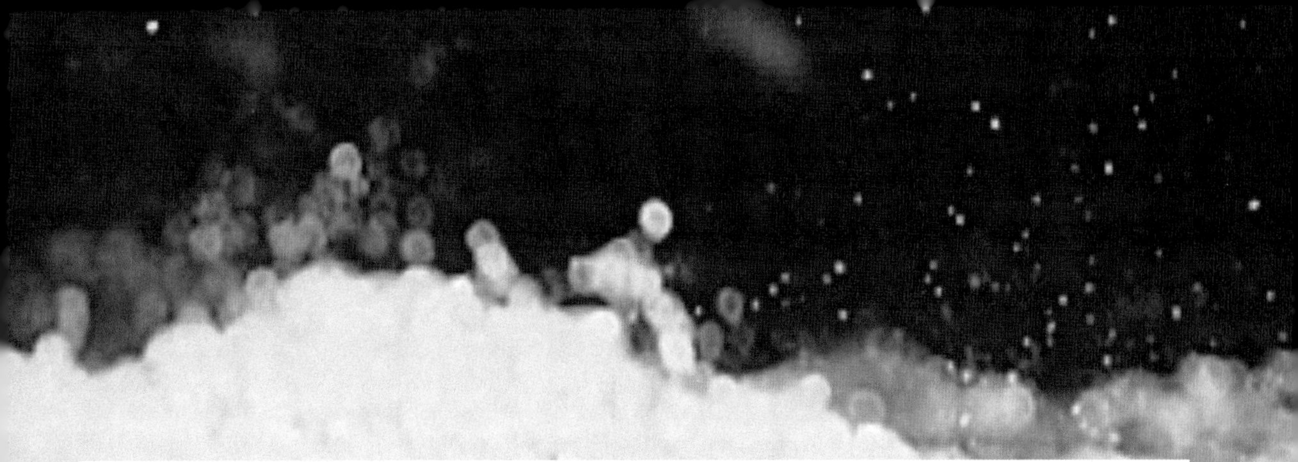

Finding Water

I desire so to invite my means of water to quench my thirst. A pasture that has been neglected far too long...

I can begin now...

Linda

11-6-11

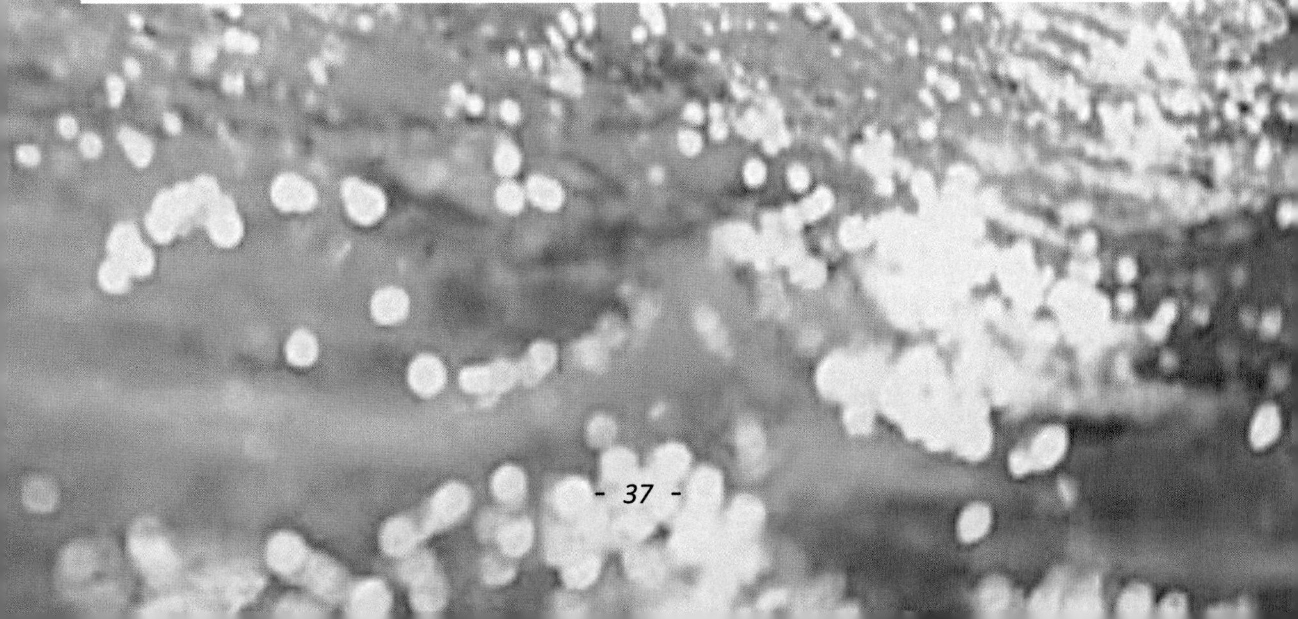

THRILLED TO BE THERE

In the expanse of snowcapped mountains
where the altitude is high
and llamas run free

Lives a woman
in an open landscape
absent automobiles and modern comforts
She walks many a muddy path
to tend to her llamas

She loves her native land
high above Quito, Ecuador
searches for any excuse not
to go into the city to sell her wares

The crowds in the market
a river of people with vibrant colors
worn by men and woman alike

There is a friendly chatter
among locals and tourists
They all respond in predictable ways
selling and buying

Off the beaten path, near the market
be surprised to stumble upon a woman
tending to her llamas
I asked the lady in broken Spanish
How old is the baby llama?
Born morning, she replied
May I take a picture?
Si
Muchas gracias

I was thrilled to be there
and chock full of adrenaline pumping happiness

Be surprised to stumble upon a woman tending to her llamas.
Otavalo Market near Quito, Ecuador.

Always a camera in hand, ready to capture an adventure.
Big Island, Hawaii

Turtles descend into the ocean, except two
they choose to be lazy and are not phased
by the crashing of the water on their rock
A hot spot feels too good, the bold ones
heads perked upright

Be still...Very still...

Green grass invites you onto a small path
The sky ice blue and not a cloud to be seen
Birds chirp above
babies cry for their mothers to feed

One with the pathway and all that exists near
A tree, hollowed out by time and seasons

Lay comfortably on lush grass
Still...Very Still

One step in front of the other, black sand between one's toes.
Punalu'u Beach, Big Island, Hawaii

A magnificence commands my attention.

In Awe

A magnificence commands my attention
Pull over... Source tells me
one footprint onto earth
A silence echoes
within whirls of wind
I stand in
Awe

Linda
01/2004

BUTTERCUP

I drove into a veterinarians parking lot
and glanced at a truck
Resting on the tailgate very quiet
a beautiful blonde Labrador

A woman held her head gently in her lap
Her touch soothed a companion
she carried in her heart for years

The Labrador's dark brown eyes met mine
a surge of energy pierced right through me

I knew ...

With tender steps, I asked the man with the yellow cap
What Is her name?

"Buttercup"
he replied with flowing tears

I imagined acres of unfenced land with endless play
pine and oak trees spoke to her...

Carefree to run through paths
layered in green meadows and streams
she left her imprint
in muddy waters

I was here
Never to be forgotten
I was loved

Buttercup's companion caressed her form
and comforted her journey home

Buttercup
left her imprint within my heart forever too...

Reflect and connect with nature's vibrations.
Oak Creek Canyon, Arizona

SOURCE OF LIFE

Fully engage in your life

Filled, every day with creative flow
from unexpected surprises and natural wonders

It is your life Source, and it will guide you

Know... how vital it is to have all your senses
activated with pleasure

Smell
Taste
Touch
Sight
Hearing

To be truly connected in your human form

Wake... thankful for all that exists
Supreme bliss from nature is Heaven
Here on earth

Be graced with Your knowing

Follow Source's lead
Delight in receiving
gentle nudges

THEY... can only offer

Becky and Linda

Allie and Linda

Three Sisters
Becky, Allie, and Linda

DEDICATION

MY SISTERS WALK WITH ME

We sail on together in different seas.
You both were the sun and the moon to me.

Now you live a sparkle
amongst the stars.

I see you, I feel you
I hear you always.

There is no greater love
than a sister's bond.
My heart aches for you,
to be here, with me.

Becky Anne
passed away at 33

Alice Andrea
passed away at 54

Far too young
when your light was taken.

You no longer have a voice
here on earth,
But I do...

I found this heart-shaped rock in the creek
the day we spread my sister Allie's ashes.
Christopher Creek, Arizona

My sister Allie

1967 - 2023

Allie's Mission Statement

If you want to find success
wherever you may go

Invest in people

They are the most important
Resource we have

If they feel valued

My sister Becky
was also a poet.

1958 - 1991

I rescued this bird and we became instant friends.

A song bird in the winter

The magic of translucent wings

Sea creatures
who live amongst the rocks

I sat with this tree talking for many days, while my sister was so sick. When I took this photo, I noticed it gave me its heart to carry with me.

Look inside the heart of a tulip.

The House of Dionysos Paphos, Cyprus
2nd century AD

The Amphitheatre of Aspendos ruins
Antalya, Turkey

Experience a smile from another.
Cairo, Egypt

Athens Olympic Museum, Greece

The gate of a fortress representing lionesses. Also a symbol of the Goddess Hera
1250 BC Mycenae, Greece

Get lost walking within a labyrinth. Maui, Hawaii

Leave your mark wherever you travel.
Oahu, Hawaii

Yosemite National Park, CA

Covering an ancient wall.
Jerusalem, Israel

Explore San Juan Islands
Washington

Live against a cliff in Rocamodour, Dordogne Region, France

Road signs will lead the way, France

Chalet in Grindelwald, Switzerland

Boys playing against a cattle water trough. Small village in Switzerland

Hand-written restaurant menu Lyon, France

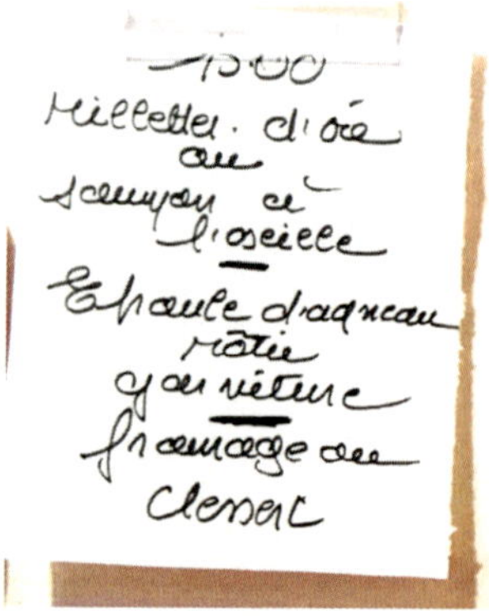

Enjoy going to school with students from Germany, Switzerland, and South Korea. Create yummy memories. Monte Carlo, Monaco

Van Gogh Museum
Amsterdam, Netherlands

Bicycle Freeways exist all over the Netherlands.

Carennac Village - France

Local man in his village
Dordogne Region, France

Elisabeth and Tomm working in the fjords
Stavanger, Norway

Enjoy a medieval pageant in Prague, Czech Republic

Walk up to the Karlstejn Castle - Czech Republic

A Viking monument
in Norway

A local artist in
Praha, Czech Republic

Sagrada Familia Church mosaic in Barcelona, Spain

The Castells are human towers for festivals in Catalonian towns in Spain

Monterey Bay Aquarium, California

Honoring those who fought in Vietnam, Washington DC

Antoni Gaudi, Spanish architect, Barcelona, Spain

Take a tour of Tuscany on a Vespa.

The magnificence of the Brunelleschi Dome, Florence, Italy

Get lost in Venice, Italy in tiny pathways and canals.

Ask a local where their favorite restaurant is, get directions and go eat there.
Pisa, Italy

Join a festival in Lucca, Italy

Menu in San Gimignano, Italy

Siena, Italy is known for its ceramics

Si Mangia Bene, good eats in Italy

The childhood home of Leonardo da Vinci. Citta da Vinci, Italy

Fields and fields of sunflowers in Tuscany

Treat yourself in Cinque Terre.

Rosslyn Chapel was founded in 1446. The ornate stone-work took my breath away. Roslin, Scotland

Robert the Bruce laid to rest here in the Abbey of Dunfermline, Scotland

Take a walk and enjoy the lavender at Trinity College, Cambridge, England.

Have some pie and gravy in a pub near Edinburgh, Scotland

The phone booth actually works!
London, England

Alaskan sea creatures

Resort in Cabo San Lucas, Mexico

Best sandwich in New Orleans, Louisiana

Sea grass near Mendocino, California

Feel the ocean's energy in Cabo San Lucas, Mexico

Meet a 1988 Olympian in Fencing, Austin Thomas, in Oranjestad, Aruba

Place your feet in soft sand, Aruba

This is a local man in traditional dress in Zakopane, Poland

A quiet moment for prayer. Poland

Search for over 600 gnome sculptures in Wroclaw, Poland

This sign screams "Never Go Backwards" Warsaw, Poland

Krakow's Market Square. Go back in time and celebrate the elegance of a carriage ride. Ask your driver to be your guide into their beautiful city. Poland

Rothenburg, Germany

A centuries-old tradition of wood-carving and fairy tale scenes like Little Red Riding Hood. Oberammergau, Germany

Children are enchanted at Tivoli Amusement Park, Copenhagen

Manneken Pis. Brussels, Belgium

Set a time for a sandwich or high tea and breathe in the colors at Tivoli Gardens. Copenhagen, Denmark

Walk into a treasure trove. Stedelijke Musea, Bruge, Belgium

A dominating glimmer over the landscape of Chamonix, France

The wonder of La Mer de Glace, a glistening ice cave. Chamonix, France

LE SOLEIL DES ALPES

Mont Blanc gives
strength in quiet moments

Le Soleil
spreading her beams
like a spider weaves its web

A dominating glimmer
over the landscape of Chamonix

Her rays sparkle through treetops
in patches of forest surrounding the village
highlighting restaurants and storefront dressings

Enter the wonder of La Mer de Glace
carved into its glacier, a glistening ice cave
avec translucent aqua drippings

Rain clouds hover
over grazing sheep in pastures
with no sense of time

Hikers, high above
their eyes, observe with reverence
as le Soleil descends...

Leaving behind an impression
delivering a farewell
for the rising midnight sun

Feel the soft earth to marching boots. The Braemar Gathering, Scottish Highland Games, in Braemar, Scotland

Come and hang out with a local. Isle of Harris, Scotland

SCOTLAND

The bagpipes arouse
your drumming heart
You cannot see enough
You cannot hear enough
Feel the soft earth
to marching boots

You will be transported back
thousands of years
Pulses of energy
vibrate from every ancient stone
There is not a rational answer
you need to be there

Be transported back thousands of years. Calanais Standing Stones erected over five thousand years ago. Isle of Lewis, Scotland

A view of Jerusalem from The Mount of Olives, Israel.

The Stone of Unction in the Church of the Holy Sepulchre, Jerusalem, Israel

ISRAEL AND PALESTINE

In June 2008, I visited Jerusalem, Israel, and Bethlehem in the West Bank of Palestine. At that time, they shared a territory. There was no fighting or war. I witnessed people practicing peace.

Church of the Nativity. Altar of the Nativity, a 14 point star grotto of the Manger. Star of David, Bethlehem, Palestine.

IRELAND

Thank you, Mary and Chris, for inviting me to stay with you in your cozy home in Tullo, County Carlow — the Celtic center of Ireland

Chris and Mary stand in front of the Cathedral window of Lonnaiocht. Eaglasta Ghleann da Loch, Glendalough. Ecclesiastical settlement. 6th century.

I am standing at a cross near Cros Chaoimhin,
St. Kevin's Cross.
Glendalough, County Wicklow, Ireland.

Circle of friends throughout the world.
We connected as students and quickly became friends.

Students from Norway, Italy, Sweden, USA, Denmark, Scotland, and Slovenia

An International School in Annecy, France. From left to right, Germany, Australia, England, Italy, Brazil, Phillipines, Ireland, USA, Germany.

United Nations, Geneva Switzerland. Students from Poland, Czech Republic, USA, Netherlands, and Spain.

CIRCLE OF FRIENDS

My home, a simple truth
with few possessions
I enfold my path
An American with a European soul

I am an artist who I believe
Inspired, with gifts from ***Source*** within

I no longer feel smothered
through life's commands that no longer serve me

Regretful shouldas and couldas

Bottom lines of a corporate world and greed

Religious perceptions and judgments

My circle of friends
liberated spirits throughout the world
Creative, and in tune
they offer assistance for me
to express in written word
through my Reflections

I am encouraged, supported
I feel Loved

Ya'axkin Butterfly Farm.
Maya Center Village,
Belize

Lake Spring -
Butterflies are abundant in
Auburn, California

TRANSFORMATION

Restless

Stirring as I grow

Thick layers protect me

Knowing not to breathe

I focus on releasing

Persistent

I am a Caterpillar

Coming out of my closed womb

"Take your first breath"

I thank thee

For assisting me

A Butterfly

FREE

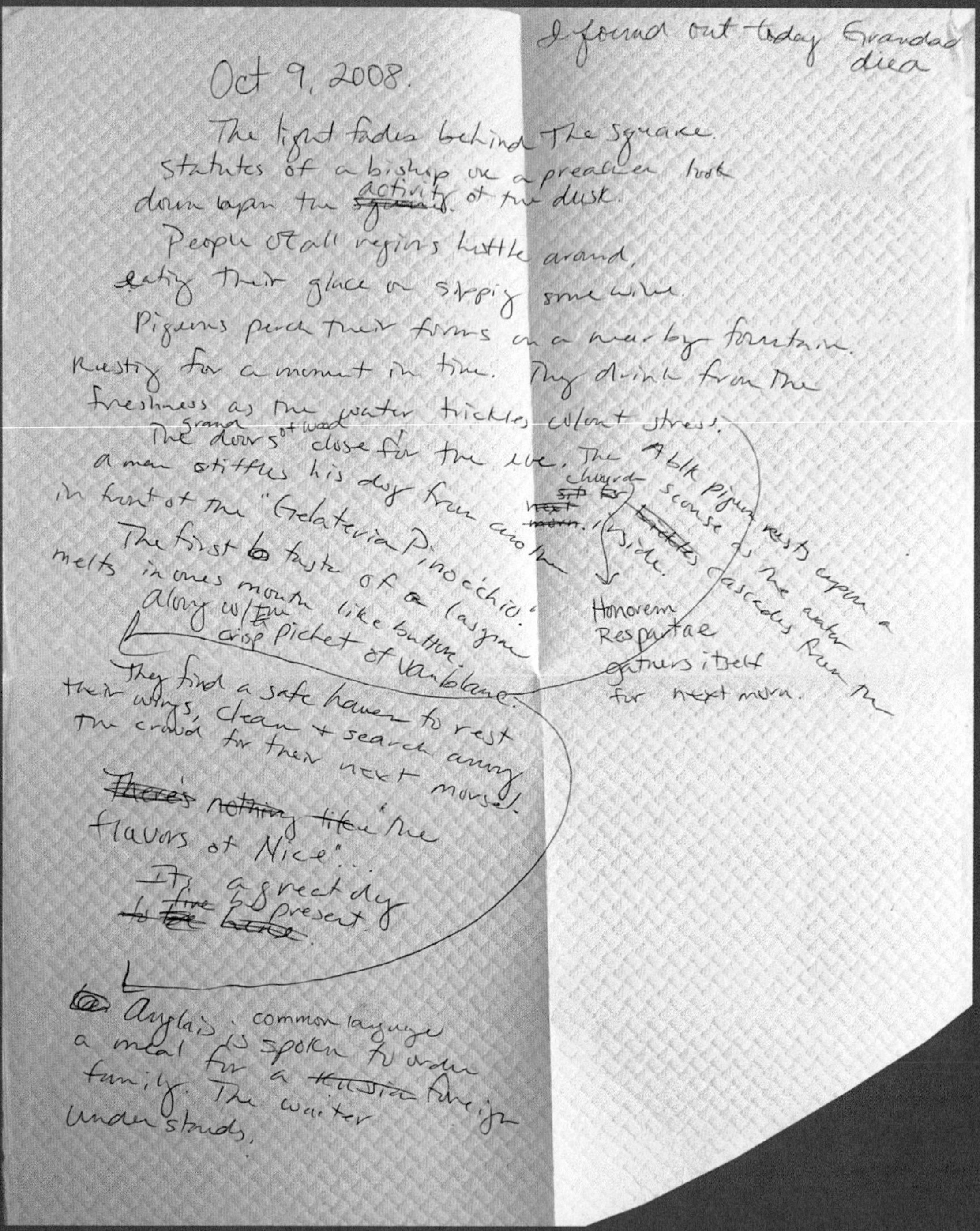

I needed a break from school and stumbled onto a beautiful cathedral. I was delighted with the activity before me. Pen in hand, I wrote this poem on a paper tablecloth. Nice, France.

FLAVORS OF NICE

The light fades behind the square
Marble statues of bishops look down
upon the activity at dusk

The ancient carved doors of
Cathedrale Sainte-Resparate
closes for the eve, priests recharge
for the coming dawn

A black pigeon plays in a nearby fountain
while others beg for a fallen treat

People of all regions, bustle around
enjoying subtle bites of glacé
and sips of vin de Blanc

A man shuffles his dog to order a scoop
in front of the Gelateria Pinocchio

The first taste of lasagna melts in my mouth like butter
accompanied with a cool pitchet de Rose'

I celebrate the life of my granddad
who passed that very day

Ever so careful not to spill onto the paper tablecloth
creating a memory with many a flowing word...

The Flavors of Nice

Millions of lights adorn the Liseberg Christmas Market.
Gothenburg, Sweden

Yes! Norwegians have reindeer boots to wear in the winter.
Stavanger, Norway

GLITTERING LIGHTS

Guided to a local village
overflowing with evening lights
that glitter

Cottages await one's arrival
rooms are touched with
alluring colors and textures
creating a cheerful comfort

A shared scrumptious meal
introduces flavors never to be forgotten

Conversations in languages spoken and unspoken
will warm your emotions... this is a promise

Creating friendships both local and abroad
for a lifetime

Who knows
where you will be guided next

Plant some seeds in a pot, in a raised bed near some trees.
Anywhere your heart desires with plenty of sunlight.
Watch them grow back year after year.

A CHERUB AMONGST WILDFLOWERS

Lovely as many
Wildflowers

Your soul is aligning
bringing you together

Prepare for the Splendor

Tommy,
You are in the Divine Realm
I heard you clearly
Through Grace

Linda

RADIANT TRUST

Calling all Angels

Beacons of Light

Hear my request

Help me Heal

My broken body
My broken mind

Protect me

Distract me
through soft music
just enough to release
the loudness out
of the stillness

Her presence speaks with compassion and strength. Glendalough, Ireland.

SURRENDER YOUR WORRIES

A pencil in hand
write down your Worries
write down your Resentments
Because, you Worry...

Humbly ask
Source, God, Higher Realms
to REMOVE these Worries and Resentments

Request a clear vision
an inspiring word perhaps
in order to REPLACE those Worries

Know this... Words are containers of energy

NOW...Rip up the pages
Rip up the pages
Rip up all the pages
You don't need to hold on to them
Anymore

Surrender them
Cleanse them with water

And so, it is Done

May you have Courage
with an inner calm
A clear vision to be in service
for yourself and others
and do it well

A young boy swings back and forth in a hammock creating waves in the sand.
White Sands on the Island of Ambergris Caye, Belize

SOFT AS SILK

A light wind flows into a blanket of palm leaves
A pleasing welcome to San Pedro, Belize

I notice a young boy
swing back and forth in a hammock
which frames his size

A subtle breeze carries his little body
creating waves in the white sand
with his fingertips

A father places his hand on a tree
I sense an anxious pose
as he contemplates into the crystal waters

I imagine his thoughts
Where did the season go?
How will I provide for my family?

He watches a youthful couple
savoring his heavenly terrain

The sun is intense
peeking, time to time
from posing puffy clouds

A father and son's footsteps
appear in powdered sand soft as silk
leaving an impression

MY LOVE

We grace each other
honoring our spirits, we merge our souls
endlessly desiring each other

I am grateful
I am aware
I am listening

I am evolving and safe
I share this with you

I know healing within me
is an absolute necessity I nurture
to renew and offer the same for you

We embrace as individuals and equal beings
To be a witness to your life
To be a witness to mine
I tear with elation of this vision

Passion, an undying regard for each other
I hold you, dear and true
Remembering many lifetimes

I hear our voices together
You are my heart

Even in interference
I feel you all-ways

I love you still...

FRISELS AND HER ORB

She arrived to me
an Ancestor in the flesh

Frisels spoke to me in play
We had a spiritual connection

Your Orb, the light
of an Angel illuminating
protection

To care for you
brought me such joy
You blessed my life with so many memories

Frisels Lee

May 2015 you were adopted from a shelter
and Squeekers became your nickname

April 2022 you passed away in my arms
Forever loved

Your companion Eastynn misses you also.

To care for you was a pleasure in my life.

The Sphinx is on the causeway leading to the Pyramid of Khafre.

Experience the intimacy of the ancient pyramids and King Tut's tomb.

FEARLESS

Escorted into Cairo, Egypt
by the military
with machine guns

It did not matter
I am Fearless

To experience the Intimacy
of the Ancient Pyramids
The Sphynx
and King Tut's Tomb

How Surreal
walking step by step into the basement
of the Egyptian Museum

Jolted back in time
from a book I studied and studied
holding each breath-taking photo
in my mind's eye

A once-in-My-lifetime Celebration
Standing in its Majesty
Tutankhamun's Sarcophagus
with Treasures in layers of Gold

In its Crowning Perfection
Becomes a part of my Eternal Soul

MARIEKE'S ADDRESS

Through her windows
admire the landscape of life in Amsterdam

Nature is exposed.
Trees are covered with moss from summers rain
Fall has touched branches with love
in order to renew

Cobblestone streets overflowing by way of bicycles
transporting people with ease

A man passes
enveloped in layers of cotton and wool
His rugged hands
confirm years of winter experience

Another quick glance
through a neighbor's window pain
Holds a sight-
Several sparkles
in dazzling colors of garnet and ginger
An open fire provides warmth

Off in the distance, a familiar bell-
the local tram signaling its next stop

A strong Ding

It's time to welcome the day.

A chilled bliss awaits

A man passes enveloped in layers of cotton and wool.
His rugged hands confirm years of winter experience.
Amsterdam, Netherlands

A mask maker at his work bench pays close attention to the details. The eyes and facial features are carefully painted with many a brush. Each mask is a unique creation. Venice, Italy

Polite conversations with smiles alike maneuver the streets ready to play their art. Harlem, New York City

A local man delicately carves his name to leave his mark of ART. Oahu, Hawaii

The natural world surrounds me, fuels my joy, opens my heart to miracles.
La Push, Washington, USA

OPEN TO MIRACLES

I am walking this earth every day
experiencing all its beauty

Within my country and abroad
I am an active participant in the
pleasures of the world

Through my natural abilities
I am creating
My Way
to be in service of self and others

The people I meet
I am welcomed…

The places I encounter
I am safe…

The comfort of my homes
I find rest…

The natural world surrounds me
fuels my joy
opens my heart to miracles

I am free to express who I am
My bravery, female essence
sustains my very existence

I am provided EVERYTHING
Through Grace…

"Free your mind
of perfection.
It does not exist"

FLAWED PAPER

The paper is flawed
Yet, it is one with the notebook

In all its flaws
A purpose to receive
A space for the words to flow
No order just ease

Red lines border the page
Break free of conditions and rules

Write beyond the red lines
Write sideways, up and down and all around
Write when you are inspired
Write when you are suffering
Write when you imagine a short sentence
Write when you feel stuck
Write when nature lightens your spirit
Write through dictation
Write your words to be sloppy
Write to be with yourself
Write without Consequences or Cares

Free your mind of Perfection
It does not exist

There is a writer inside you
A masterpiece to be created

I THINK OF INGRID

Gazing out a picture framed window on a soft cushy seat
in the lobby of the Clarion Hotel Post
offering a view of life in Goteborg, Sweden full of Wonder

A man passes by on a bicycle holding a broken umbrella
at a smooth pace, not a care in the world
A row of bicycles layered in white powder
black coats and hoodies cover those fighting the snow

Followed by a shot of Schnapps and SKÅL!

Ingrid and Thore, Thank you for welcoming me into your family

A feast indeed prepared by Anne and Bert

A local fish market Goteborg, Sweden

It's Easter Sunday, a celebration with
decorative eggs hang from twigs in color as is tradition
Tulips in a vase, Ingrid in a soft pink blouse and Thore
happily displaying a yellow and green bunny napkin

Playing in the background
was the same album and excitement
where I was welcomed at their Christmas celebration nine years earlier
A traditional song to toast and sing by the family
followed by a shot of Schnapps and SKÅL !!

A feast indeed prepared by Anne and Bert
Herring with honey mustard sauce on toast
cream colored butter cheese spread on top a cracker
presented upon plates, a wedding gift sixty years ago

Sliced lamb, rosemary and garlic backed to perfection
Potatoes with onions, leeks and cream
fresh snap green beans, flavors melt in my mouth
followed by a shot of Schnapps and SKÅL !!

Laughter and fellowship, memories of Milan, Italy
where the bond of a lasting friendship began
Ohhh Milano, a tribute with Limoncello and SKÅL !!
followed by an ice cream treat with raspberries
olive oil and salt...Delicious

I love you Linda
Ingrid and I hold each other tight; I love you more Ingrid
I fulfilled a longing, the tender care of a mother
Our hearts met again my sweet Ingrid

Whenever I would house sit for my friend Jan, Miss Mini and I always had an understanding. Bliss from the outdoors and exploring.
Northern California

MISS MINI'S PORCH

Her courtyard is active with life

Bees are engaged
pollinating
one blossom to another

Squirrels perch on a sturdy branch
contemplating their next nibble

Mushroom caps arise
from layers of dormant grass and leaves

A fountain provides water to winged friends
A refreshing soak with play

Deer affirm a desired tranquility
laying content beneath
oak trees with "eyes"

Vines cascade in variations of green
hugging the black railing –
connecting grapes soon to follow

Miss Mini arrives from an adventure
a petite ball of fluff
squinting her yellow eyes
she gazes towards the sun

A catnap beckons ...

A local man watches and waits to provide his feathered friends a safe passage.
River Thiou, Annecy, France

LOVE'S WINGED MESSENGERS

A nest, warm with love of mother

A crack in its shell

Breaks free

Naked helpless and hungry

Eyelids remain closed

With awkward movements

In time, it's vision

Opens to a colorful world

Encouraged to venture

Given a chance to fly

A man watches and waits

Patiently for the day

He can provide his feathered friends

A safe passage

My dearest friend, a privilege to be your guide through six countries while you were still able to see a little color.
Lisse, Netherlands

Feast your eyes on colorful fireworks and rainbow rows of Dutch tulips.
Keukenhof Tulip Market, Lisse, Netherlands

MARY

Seeing what you cannot see
Black and white, squares and circles
of color coming in through a tiny pin dot

I am honored you trusted me, felt safe
to guide you through 6 countries
being brave and unstoppable
to fully experience anew

Visiting The Keukenhof Tulip Market
it was my pleasure to describe
each family of tulips
I watched as you savored and feasted on
colorful fireworks and rainbow layers
between Dutch tulips

Returning home your touch places each broken
piece of tile with ease
within your mind onto a blank board
creating a mosaic masterpiece

Every day you imagine your world
living through your senses
in vivid color and textures

TO COMPARE

One cannot referee
an experience to another

C'est ma Vie

Every struggle or savior faire creates change

Each experience requires
understanding of self

Each layer is meant to come forth
to be healed

Feeling judged hurts deeply

There is no comparison in growth

UNWAVERING RIVER

A twig, a boulder
A dam of branches from a fallen tree
being one with the flow of the river

Obstacles have no ability to stop the current.

Water barrels right through,
any debris left behind in scattered pieces.

Yet… all the currents are flowing
the same direction with one goal.

LIFE

Providing a consistent sustenance
to trees and foliage close by

Animals partake in a drink,
dampened their fur from its mist.

Fish and insects both active
as they nibble and swim.

Delicate rocks and boulders provide streams
that shift into small waterfalls.

Let's ponder…

Without debris, how would you hear
A rivers roar
A streams ripple
A soft trickle from a brook

It is unwavering love for you

West Fork Trail,
Sedona, Arizona

A single sunflower from a seed dropped by a bird. A moth appeared and stayed long enough for me to get my camera.

For McKenna

Standing on the deck
of a cruise ship
in the middle of
The Caribbean Sea

A butterfly lands on a rail
wings wide enough
to hold its tiny body

We say hello…
then disappeared on a puff of air

I believe
Loved ones that have passed
can appear to us
in celestial forms sending a message
here on earth

I sensed it was McKenna
Mac was her nickname

The short visit made
my heart full
To know she is finally
Free
from suffering

"May you be filled with loving kindness

May you be well...

May you be peaceful and at ease

May you be happy"

Linda Lee

January 2, 2003

I love finding a story on my nature walks.
A happy face showed itself on the bloom of a barrel cactus.
Bahamas

Where are you heading next?

ACKNOWLEDGMENTS

I have been deeply nourished by many who have touched my life because all healing, inspiration and bravery happens in relationships.
Thank you for encouraging me and believing in my written words. You've taught me, challenged me and walked beside me.

Tina, for your Native American wisdom and insight into my soul. We share a similar childhood; you understand me with compassion. I am proud to call you sister. You have a writing gift that needs to be on paper. I am here for you.

Maurice, your guidance and expertise in business helped mold my company, Hope with Helpers into a resource based in Hope and Bravery.

Dan, you weathered many a storm with me. Your patience and listening with love helped me to feel safe and I adore you.

Meredith, I always felt your acceptance, love and Oscars too.

Heather, when you finish your first book don't forget to dance a Jig like we use to. Now get going Little One.

Profound gratitude for my sisters Becky and Allie. You gave me strength and determination my message would be heard. I felt you always speaking to me from the spiritual realm. My heart aches for you. There is an emptiness without you both here.

For Ingrid and Trees, you both showed me what is felt like to have a mother who knew how to love. My life is possible because of your love even in the spiritual realm.

A heartfelt thanks to Margaret, your support in the creation of my book. Your creative gifts are astounding. Mila, your writing coach wisdom and knowledge of KDP.

For Bobbi, Todd and Kelly and everyone who appears in this book, named and unnamed, thank you for being my reflection.

And finally, for my nature family, I am so blessed you showed me as a child to hear you, see your energy and most of all taught me that we are all connected.

DID YOU LEAVE A REVIEW?

As a self-published author,
reviews are what keeps
REFLECTIONS
Growing.

If you found my book inspiring
and helpful, please leave me
a review on Amazon.com
Your review helps other people
find this book and hopefully
Live their Brave.

I promise to read every single review.

ABOUT THE AUTHOR

Linda Lee is an author, photographer, educator and lover of travel and nature's wisdom.

She experienced her first Solo travel at 16 being a foreign exchange student in Best, Netherlands. That early awareness profoundly changed her, a passion emerged.

She has traveled 32 countries and every state except North and South Carolina, which she plans to visit soon!

Linda satisfies her creative spirit and insatiable curiosity by documenting her journeys through her photography and written word.

In 2008, she decided to follow her own lead by leaving the corporate world and move back to Europe where it all began. She sold everything she owned and moved to France. During her travels abroad she established meaningful connections and found herself immersed in cross-cultural experiences.

Linda is an advocate for people living with C-PTSD

She is focused on widespread education to cultivate mental wellbeing. This knowledge is providing a better understanding of childhood trauma.

Linda currently lives in Northern California, with nature's essence surrounding her.

These bountiful attributes and travel are Linda's wellspring.

To learn more about Linda,
visit her website
HopeWithHelpers.com

Made in the USA
Las Vegas, NV
27 October 2025

33079508R00086